The Archival Advantage: Integrating Archival Expertise into Management of Born-digital Library Materials

Jackie Dooley

OCLC Research

OCLC Research
Dublin, Ohio 43017 USA
www.oclc.org

ISBN: 1-55653-495-7 (978-1-55653-495-9)
OCLC Control Number: 911139101

Please direct correspondence to:
Jackie Dooley
Program Officer
dooleyj@oclc.org

Suggested citation:
Dooley, Jackie. 2015. *The Archival Advantage: Integrating Archival Expertise into Management of Born-digital Library Materials*. Dublin, Ohio: OCLC Research.
http://www.oclc.org/content/dam/research/publications/2015/oclcresearch-archival-advantage-2015.pdf.

Contents

Acknowledgments

Many colleagues generously contributed their time to review drafts of this essay, and their feedback was invaluable.

The external reviewers were Carly Dearborn (Purdue University), Nancy Enneking (Getty Research Institute), Ricc Ferrante (Smithsonian Institution), Ben Goldman (Pennsylvania State University), Mark Greene (University of Wyoming), Peter Hirtle (Cornell University and Harvard University), Matthew McKinley (University of California, Irvine), Naomi Nelson (Duke University), Erin O'Meara (Gates Archive), Susan Parker (University of California, Los Angeles), Sarah Pritchard (Northwestern University), Gabriela Redwine (Yale University), Anne Sauer (Cornell University), Alice Schreyer (University of Chicago), Seth Shaw (Clayton State University), Cyndi Shein (University of Nevada, Las Vegas), Rob Spindler (Arizona State University), and Dave Thompson (Wellcome Library).

OCLC Research colleagues who offered feedback are Ricky Erway, Constance Malpas, Merrilee Proffitt, Jennifer Schaffner, Karen Smith-Yoshimura, and Roy Tennant.

Heartfelt thanks to you all!

Introduction

Archivists[1] and special collections librarians bring unique expertise to the management of digitally created research library materials, both during the planning and policy development stages and at other key points throughout the acquisition-to-access life cycle. Successful digital programs and projects inevitably involve a disparate cast of characters, and administrative boundaries are sometimes permeated. Working in collaboration with other library specialists, archivists can uniquely contribute to the success of digital initiatives.

Archivists use the term "born digital" rather than "digital" for materials that are created and managed in digital form.[2] The more generic term "digital" can also refer to digitized materials and formally published digital resources such as e-journals and music CDs. Both terms are used in this essay as appropriate for the particular context.

Many archivists manage born-digital archival materials that clearly fall within their traditional collecting purview. These include digital content acquired from literary authors, scholars, university offices, and private organizations, often received together with analog materials (these are referred to as "hybrid collections"). These archivists have developed new skills and knowledge that help further translate their "traditional" expertise with analog materials into the digital realm.[3]

This essay argues for involving archivists in management of other types of materials that may have less obvious archival characteristics such as research data, email, and websites. Some are in digital formats that lack clear analog equivalents (e.g., blogs, Twitter, wikis, software) and now are within the scope of what research libraries should document and preserve. Much of what was considered "grey literature" in the print context is now digital. The scholarly and cultural records are becoming more complex as evidence, methodology, and discussion join more traditional outputs.[4]

The essay includes an overview of some characteristics of archival materials and born-digital resources to provide context.

The core of the essay illuminates ten areas of archival expertise and their relevance to the digital context. These areas include appraising the significance of content, documenting the context of creation, negotiating with collection donors and nurturing these relationships over time, recognizing and navigating legal issues, and using practical approaches to creating metadata for large collections. Each of these is equally relevant for digital and analog (physical) materials. In-depth knowledge of each area helps ensure that the right questions are addressed.

The intended audience for this essay encompasses the wide variety of library specialists who may be involved in digital programs and projects, particularly library directors and other managers who set the vision and direction for digital initiatives. Others include technology specialists who manage systems and services in areas such as repository design, hardware and software management, digitization, and website development; data curation experts; digital preservationists who contribute their understanding of the functional and technical requirements for reliable long-term protection of content; liaison librarians who have close relationships with researchers and knowledge of research methods; and metadata specialists. Some of these actors may have expertise that overlaps with that of archivists.

Archivists too may find value in the explanations of the ten areas of archival expertise and the arguments for including archivists in a wide range of digital initiatives.

Characteristics of Archival Materials

Archivists have long been responsible for managing primary source collections in analog form. Examples include personal manuscript collections; research data recorded in laboratory or field notebooks; correspondence and office records acquired from university officials; photographs that document daily life; and brochures and other ephemera produced by organizations and government agencies in the course of their work.

What are some of the innate characteristics of archival materials and their management that differentiate them relative to general library holdings and require a specialized skill set?

- Most are unique and unpublished; they originate from a single source, and "originals" exist in a single location.

- While published materials inherently are publicly available, few archival materials can be made accessible until they have been acquired by an archive, organized, and made discoverable.

- Only a small percentage of unique materials warrant acquisition by a library or archive. Not every person, organization, or topic is important enough to be documented over the long term.

- Items within collections can lose much of their meaning if the broader context of creation and original use is missing. Archival materials are managed as organic collections, not as individual items.

- A collection can be enormous. For example, the papers of an elected official, a university president, or a large commercial firm can contain millions of items.

- Aspects of copyright law differ from published materials.

- The owning institution must actively manage multiple aspects of intellectual property.

- Privacy considerations must be mitigated.

- Manuscripts and other materials can be subtly forged or altered. Creators or donors can bowdlerize a collection, sometimes for the purpose of protecting reputation or privacy.

- Relationships with donors are carefully established prior to acquisition and nurtured over time.

- Most archival materials are retained permanently, in contrast with general collections, which periodically are weeded of materials that no longer serve user needs. The need for reappraisal in some cases is, however, increasingly being recognized.

- A single collection may grow over time as new material is accessioned, requiring additional processing and changes to metadata.

- Due to their unique nature, archival materials are stored and made accessible under secure conditions.

- Responsibility for preservation of published materials may be shared across a community, while the custodian of archival originals usually is uniquely responsible.

- The standard descriptive data elements that are found on published materials often do not appear on archival materials.

- Archival collections are more likely to be described using collection-level metadata rather than at the item level, as is done for general library holdings.

Most of these characteristics are equally relevant in both analog and digital contexts, though a new array of twists applies for digital resources.

Characteristics of Born-digital Materials

The content and format of born-digital materials that research libraries acquire cover a broad spectrum. Depending on the nature of the material, approaches to acquisition, management, and access may differ. This brief table of selected types of material illustrates parallels between analog and digital versions:

Type Of Material	Sample Analog Formats	Sample Digital Formats
Architectural records	Blueprints, elevations, renderings	CAD files
Audio recordings	Tapes, LPs, wax cylinders	CDs, digital sound files
Correspondence	Letters	Email, word processing files, social media
Data	Lab notebooks, logbooks, ledgers	Spreadsheets, databases
Institutional records	Typed or printed documents	Word processing files, PDFs, databases
Manuscripts	Handwritten or typed documents, diaries	Word processing files, Facebook posts, blogs
Moving images	Film, video	DVDs, digital video files
Organizational publications	Brochures, newsletters, reports	Websites, desktop publishing files
Photographs	Film-based media such as prints, negatives, slides	Digital image files, Flickr, Instagram photos

Archives collect all types of material listed in the left column. Unpublished materials in analog formats (middle column) typically are acquired via the usual archival channels, such as individual donors or offices of the local institution. They are placed in archival custody under controlled-access conditions due to their physical nature, need for security, and other special characteristics.

Many materials in digital formats (right column) also have archival characteristics. Materials in many of these formats would benefit from including archivists in their management, whether or not the archives is the custodial department.

Contrast this with the broader library collection of digital materials that have been published in the traditional sense of having been selected, edited, and formally issued in mass copies. These include e-journals, e-books, music CDs, DVDs, and digital games. Such materials have no archival characteristics.

The following examples serve to illustrate ways in which archivists' expertise comes into play in management of selected types of born-digital materials:

Websites: In many research libraries, responsibility for web harvesting is distributed: government information librarians collect political campaign or government agency content; subject specialists harvest sites important to their academic disciplines; institutional archivists harvest the web domain of their home institution. Ideally, they acquire web materials that fit with broader selection policies of the custodial unit.[5]

Web content often is considered published, but the U.S. Copyright Office maintains that this is rarely so because very few website owners make their sites available for wholesale download[6] (an obscure distinction, perhaps, to all but copyright attorneys). This is significant in terms of legal protections if website owners do not register their sites with the Copyright Office. Other archival characteristics of websites include their size and complexity, their frequently changing content, the need to negotiate terms with the owner (if the content is to be made publicly accessible by the library), the significance of the context of creation, the absence of sufficient identifying information, and the nature of collection-level metadata.

Although harvesting has become widespread, the amount of content being preserved overall is small relative to the universe of content that warrants it. Until harvesting is done at scale, massive quantities of formerly analog archival material that is no longer issued in print will be lost. Research libraries must step up activity in this area.[7]

Research Data: Management of scholarly research data has become a central concern for research libraries now that funding agencies are issuing mandates requiring public access to data.[8] Libraries that have established data curation centers are assisting faculty with interpreting and adhering to these relatively new requirements, such as by helping to craft the data management plans required by granting agencies.[9] Some aspects of these plans map easily to the archival skills detailed in this essay: these include appraising content, documenting context, preparing metadata, identifying the need for restrictions, and helping determine the warranted duration of retention.

To date, including archivists on data management teams is the exception rather than the rule. Purdue University[10] is one example of a data repository in which archivists play key roles, such as routinely assisting researchers with the above-listed activities and articulating the requirements of digital preservation.[11]

Email: Information technology departments rightfully are the custodians of active organizational email. In some institutions, policy is to retain email for a specified period of time and then delete it en masse without considering long-term value; in others, records management schedules apply and govern retention of particular email (whether or not these are adhered to is another matter). Commercial email services in the cloud have a variety of policies for length or selectivity of retention, but individual or organizational subscribers do not control those policies.[12] Many firms sell software products for management of email that permit actions such as selective retention based on specified characteristics,[13] but use of these is uncommon across the research library sector.

Given that email is today's primary means of corresponding, deleting all email that is more than a few years old eliminates a significant element of personal and organizational history. Many government agencies are mandated to preserve email and so must put an email management system in place, often under the supervision of the jurisdictional archives (local, state, or national).

Archives in research libraries sometimes acquire email as part of a personal or organizational collection. The archival profession has focused significant attention on developing practices for email identification, ingest, preservation, and access.[14]

Ten Areas of Archival Expertise

As noted, most issues that archivists contend with in the analog environment pertain equally in the digital realm. This section outlines ten key areas of archival expertise,[15] each of which has complex dimensions and is followed by sample questions illustrating issues that can arise when acquiring and managing born-digital materials (some of these questions are equally applicable to analog materials). Archivists' experience gives them insight into answers to these questions.

Such questions must be addressed, if not by an archivist on the team, then by others who will need to become well versed in archival issues and solutions.

1. Ownership

The issue: Legal ownership of the digital property.

Most physical property is legally owned by someone, whether a person or an organization. This is an issue that archivists confront every time they seek or are offered a collection. When the chain of custody (see Authenticity) isn't clear, the archivist opens a conversation about who has the legal standing to donate or sell materials. It sometimes happens that a person or organization offers a donation without knowing whether they are in fact the legitimate owner. Negotiating donations of any type also may involve a variety of sensitivities that archivists handle on a routine basis (see Donor Relations).

Within the college or university context, complexities may exist with regard to ownership of faculty research and teaching files because it is not always clear whether they are considered official university records. Some universities consider them the personal property of the faculty member, in which case a deed of gift is necessary. Files relating to a faculty member's administrative duties, however—such as department chair or chair of a university committee—are usually considered official and are governed by the university's records retention schedule.

For most private donations, a deed of gift should be executed to provide legal evidence of the donation (see Transfer of Ownership). Within an organization such as a university, a less formal transfer form is used for sending official records to the institutional archives.

Sample questions:

- When the creator of personal digital materials is deceased, and there are either multiple heirs or no known heirs, how do we determine who has the right to donate?

- Who has the right to donate organizational records? The CEO of a commercial firm? The director of a nonprofit organization? The heirs of an employee who took materials home upon retirement?

- Which inactive records must be retained for legal purposes by an organization that still exists?

- Who owns digital research data? The researcher? The university? The government agency that funded it?

- What does "ownership" mean when it's so easy to make identical copies of digital files?

2. Donor Relations

The issue: Factors to address when working with donors of digital content.

Archivists are expert in establishing strong relationships with donors, negotiating terms, raising legal issues, and discussing sensitive topics. They recognize that the donation of private papers can be a very personal experience. Institutional archivists often must educate administrators and staff about the importance and benefits of transferring material to the repository. Some donors and creators ask pointed questions about how the institution will manage the materials. Some may have strong preferences about access. Relationships with many donors continue for years and must be nurtured to ensure the institution's positive reputation as a desirable home for others' materials.

In working with donors of all types, archivists discuss the scope of materials that have sufficient value to be placed in the archives (see Appraisal). Large organizations usually have records retention schedules that stipulate which types of office records have permanent value and should be transferred to the archives when the materials are no longer actively used.[16] Typically, a small percentage of the records created are designated for transfer to the archives.

These issues, and many more, are equally relevant when the material being considered for donation is digital. The conversation must cover a wide range of the creator's practices.[17] Archivists explore with the donor issues such as types of hardware and software used, file naming conventions, email retention practices, migration of files from one computer and file format to the next, and participation in social media. Email systems, sensitive content, versioning, backup, accounts, passwords and security are other important topics.

Sample questions:

- Should we ask the donor whether anyone else has copies of all or significant portions of the digital material?

- Do we have to consult the donor before we recover deleted files?

- Is it necessary to obtain passwords?

- What questions should we ask related to personally identifiable information that may be in digital organizational records?

- May the donor take a tax deduction for a digital donation?

- If we choose not to retain some material after acquiring it, how do we negotiate this with the donor?

- With whom do we discuss these issues if the creator is deceased?

- Which of the above questions pertain to website owners?

3. Intellectual Property

The issue: Legal ownership of the intellectual property rights associated with the material.

Ownership of intellectual property rights is completely distinct from ownership of physical property, and the two often are owned by different entities. For example, an archive may own a collection of papers, but the author may retain copyright in the manuscripts and correspondence that he authored. The rights dictated by U.S. law include publication, distribution, reproduction and others.[18]

For an archivist, explaining intellectual property to donors is routine. Few creators realize that they own copyright in their own unpublished writings, let alone that provisions of copyright law differ for unpublished and published material.[19] Archivists advise donors on issues such as the materials in which they do and do not hold the rights, as well as factors to weigh in deciding whether to retain or transfer rights. Most collections include writings by multiple people, each of whom likely owns her own copyrights. These issues are equally germane whether negotiating acquisition with a person or an organization.

As with the material itself, it is important to address ownership of intellectual property in the deed of gift (see Transfer of Ownership).

Sample questions:

- What are the essential points to make to digital donors who aren't familiar with copyright basics?

- What happens if the donor doesn't know who holds copyright?

- Must the copyright status of every single item in a collection be investigated?

- Can digital materials be orphan works?

- Should the library attempt to obtain copyright to the digital content? Does this simplify or complicate management of a collection?

- Are there intellectual property issues associated with making an author's email available via the Internet?

- What is the duration of copyright for an undated website?

- Who owns the copyright in digital photographs taken for an organization by a freelance photographer?

- Does the university own the copyright in digital recordings of a conference or poetry reading series? What about oral histories?

4. Appraisal

The issue: Significance of the material in the context of the institution's collecting mission.

In the archival context, appraisal is the process of determining whether or not materials have legal, informational, or other types of value.[20] Appraisal should take place within a larger institutional mission and collecting policy. The value may be specific to the institution that acquires the material or may apply more generally to society at large. This evaluation includes consideration of the ways in which the material might be used over time. Archival appraisal in this respect typically is not concerned with monetary value.[21]

Appraisal may take place at one or more stages in the process of acquiring and managing the materials, such as prior to negotiating with the donor or after materials have been accessioned and are processed for preservation and use. The basis of any appraisal decision usually involves multiple factors; no single consideration is likely to determine whether the materials will be acquired or retained.

A collection that contains born-digital materials is appraised prior to acquisition in the aggregate, based in part on the context of creation, the same as analog materials. It may not be possible to evaluate the detailed content until a later point, however; digital tools fit-to-purpose must be used to examine them in order to avoid damage or inadvertent alteration of the content (see Permanence).

Sample questions:

- Does the born-digital material fit our collection development policy? If not, can we help the donor by identifying a better home for it?

- Should we acquire an author's digital files if we already have corresponding paper manuscripts for all or some of the content?

- Should we accept multiple copies of digital files?

- No documentation accompanied these scientific data sets. How do we know whether the data warrant preservation?

- How do we determine whether the content is of value if the software used to create it is obsolete?

- Do digital materials have monetary value?

- Should we consider the high cost of processing materials in obsolete digital formats as part of the appraisal decision?

5. Context of Creation and Use

The issue: The circumstances under which the materials were produced and their relationship to the creator's overall output.

An archival collection typically consists of a body of materials that is meaningful in the aggregate, more so than as individual items. The context of that material is comprised of the circumstances surrounding its creation, ownership, custody, and intended use. All of these inform an archivist's understanding of the material so that its full significance can be determined and the context itself can be understood and preserved. An understanding of context is critical in just about every stage of archival management, from preliminary investigation of an acquisition to processing the materials and creating metadata.

Here are some examples of how context adds meaning: A printout of one email message to or from a government official may completely misrepresent the agency's response to an issue in the absence of the related messages and documents that elaborate the circumstances. A scholar cannot properly evaluate one version of an author's manuscript without reading it in the context of other versions and associated materials. The evolving demographic profile of a company's employees can be studied only if a broad swath of corporate data can be examined longitudinally. Survey data lacks meaning if not accompanied by the researcher's codebook. Constituent correspondence received at the district office of a member of Congress presents a partial view of community relations unless studied in the context of materials received by the member's Washington D.C. office.

Sample questions:

- What information is necessary to provide sufficient context for a scientist's data sets?

- Is it possible to determine context if the digital collection is incomplete?

- What sort of contextual information is needed for a website?

- For organizational records, what does the function of the office of origin imply about the significance of its records?

- Is it relevant to know whether the duties of a staff member who donated digital office records changed over time? Or whether the functions of the office changed?

- What is the appropriate amount of biographical information to establish context for a collection of personal digital materials?

- Is context always important?

6. Authenticity

The issue: Factors that help determine whether the materials can serve as an accurate, reliable record of the creator's output.

An authentic document is complete and unchanged; it has not been subject to forgery, manipulation, or any other type of alteration since it left the creator's custody. Accuracy is of course desirable in general, but authenticity is particularly critical when a document becomes evidence in a legal proceeding. U.S. rules of evidence stipulate that, to be presumed authentic, documents must be created in the normal course of business (or other human activity), and there can be no overt reason to suspect their trustworthiness.[22] Authenticity is also essential for government records so that the public can have confidence that the records they use are exactly the ones that were generated.

Documenting the chain of custody from creation to acquisition helps determine whether materials are genuine and free from tampering. By definition, the final version owned by the creator is authentic. The authenticity of analog materials is usually presumed, rather than requiring affirmation, unless suspicions are aroused. A conversation with the donor about ownership usually reveals information about the chain of custody since the material was created.

Digital files can be altered far more easily than their analog equivalents. Changes may be accidental: for example, library or archives staff can inadvertently alter documents if they have not been properly trained. The mere act of opening a file can alter the bits and change the content. Resaving a document alters the date of last use, which can obscure the creator's own record of use. Such alterations can be revealed when software tools are applied to determine whether a document matches the version that was originally acquired. Digital tools can be used to check for fixity of the content.[23] Duplication of files during processing, migration of file formats, and other aspects of digital management must be done in a manner that does not threaten authenticity.

Sample questions:

- How do we determine the chain of custody since the materials were created?

- Can we consider an organizational document to be authentic if we didn't acquire it from the office of origin?

- Is a digital document considered authentic if the donor's representative inadvertently altered it?

- Are the copies that we make for digital processing and preservation considered authentic?

7. Restrictions on Access and Use

The issue: Limitations on access to or use of materials.

Archivists must determine whether statutes or the donor's wishes dictate that access to certain types of material be restricted; the former pertains principally to organizational records. U.S. federal law mandates certain restrictions (such as student records governed by FERPA,[24] or medical records governed by HIPAA[25]). State laws (such as California's Public Records Act)[26] usually dictate that most government records must be accessible to the public on request but that others may be restricted (such as active legal cases to which the state is party, active criminal investigations, and personally identifying information such as addresses and Social Security numbers).

In addition to legally mandated restrictions, donors sometimes wish to impose their own restrictions on access, often for reasons of personal or family privacy. Good archival practice is to accept such restrictions for as brief a time period as possible (such as ten years or the person's lifetime) and to ensure that there is a definitive, easily identified end date. If the type and length of restrictions cannot be agreed upon, it may not be appropriate to acquire the materials.

Two common types of restriction on use relate to making copies and quoting content; in such situations, familiarity with intellectual property issues is essential. As with restrictions on access, archives may decline to acquire a collection if the donor insists on use restrictions that are seen as unreasonable or that violate institutional policy.

In the digital realm, administering restrictions is far more complex than it is for analog materials. Although it is logical to assume that digital materials should be available anywhere rather than from a single physical location, the need to isolate personally identifying information, manage restrictions, prevent alteration of content, limit copying, and address legal issues has led many archives to restrict use to the physical reading room or a "virtual reading room" of some kind.[27] A recent controversy at the University of Oregon concerning the release of 22,000 email messages from the university president's office without having been vetted by the university archives has dramatically demonstrated the challenges involved.[28]

Sample questions:

- What types of archival materials are most likely to contain content that may require restriction?

- Can all of a creator's digital data be made publicly available if no restrictions were specified?

- Under what circumstances can medical research data be made public?

- May university officials restrict access to their digital correspondence?

- Are there issues associated with providing digital access to papers written by students as course assignments?

- Is it possible to automate review of born-digital materials for sensitive material such as Social Security numbers? What's the next step if we find some?

- How are time-limited restrictions managed?

8. Transfer of Ownership

The issue: Terms and conditions to be discussed at the point of transferring ownership to the institution.

Just as archivists negotiate issues related to initial ownership of materials, they oversee the process of transferring ownership to the institution via a deed of gift.

The essential function of a deed of gift is to effect change of ownership of property, whether physical or digital, from the existing owner to the acquiring institution. Without a deed, the possibility exists that misunderstandings may arise in the future, such as if an heir were to question the institution's right to keep the materials. A deed is a contract establishing the conditions governing transfer of title to both the materials and the intellectual property (the latter may either be retained by the donor or transferred to the institution).

The deed may be simple or complex, depending on the circumstances. It should clearly state that the materials will be open for public access in accord with the institution's policies, as well as that the institution may make analog and digital copies for preservation and public access. The deed should address any restrictions on reproduction, access, or use; delivery to the institution; and disposition of any materials that the institution does not consider to have research value.

Model deeds have been developed to address such considerations such as those developed by the Association of Research Libraries.[29]

Sample questions:

- By what means should digital files be transferred from donor to the institution?

- Should analog and digital materials be addressed separately and/or differently in the deed of gift?

- Is a deed of gift needed for a professor's research data?

- Is it acceptable if the donor wants to keep a copy of some of all of the material?

9. Permanence

The issue: Preservation of the authentic materials into the foreseeable future.

Years may pass between the time of creation of born-digital materials and their acquisition by an institution. When this is case, further delay in processing and preserving them is risky. The content may become unusable due to obsolescence of hardware and/or software, and physical media may degrade to the point that recovery is impossible. Opening digital files for inspection of content may not be feasible before the acquisition decision is made. The procedures for inspection and management can be complex and costly. Archivists who learn techniques for processing born-digital materials know how to deal with these issues, including selection and use of tools for safe processing.[30] Routine back-up procedures are not sufficient to preserve authenticity of content and permanent validity of digital files. IT staff, digital preservation experts, and archivists working in tandem can select and implement appropriate systems and procedures.

Not all materials in a digital repository may warrant the permanent retention that is typical for analog archival materials; "forever" may not be feasible, given the complexities of storing, migrating and auditing files over time. Research libraries deaccession analog books and serials that are no longer considered important enough to warrant precious shelf space. Analog archival materials are sometimes reappraised and deaccessioned as well.[31]

Will we begin to see similar decisions made for digital materials? The evaluation and reappraisal processes that archivists conduct will be important in making such decisions.

Research data present an interesting case. Data management plans play a role in determining retention periods, and library staff may be called upon for advice. Given how recently data management requirements have emerged, the questions are numerous, complex, and mostly unresolved. Regardless, the attendant issues will be familiar to archivists.

Sample questions:

- What is an appropriate—and realistic—retention period for this born-digital material?

- Should we continue devoting server space to material that has received little if any use?

- If standard back-up systems aren't sufficient for preserving files over the long term, what type of environment meets digital preservation standards?

- What is a "clean workstation"?

- Should we retain the physical media on which the library has acquired born-digital material after the content has been copied during processing?

- How can we preserve content that was created using obsolete hardware, software, and file formats?

- Should all files be migrated to current versions of software?

- Will our institutional preservation strategy require changes to ensure persistence of these digital resources?

10. Collection-Level Metadata

The issue: Efficient creation of contextual and descriptive metadata for discovery and access.

Collection-level description is the archival norm. It is far more efficient than item-level description, and it is more effective because the context in which the materials were created and used is part of the description. Consider a U.S. Senator's papers encompassing two million items, or a documentary photographer's career output that includes many similar images created during each photo shoot, or the minutes of an organization's board meetings over the course of decades. For such materials, item-level description would be both unmanageable and unnecessary.

Many archival materials do not explicitly include any of the identifying data elements that typically appear on published items (e.g., creator, title, date, extent). Archivists organize and analyze material for which identification of basic data points and detailed description can come only from the broader context in which the material was created and used. A collection-level summary typically captures context, creator name, formats, dates, extent of the materials, associated names, and more. If the material is voluminous or requires a deeper description, the archivist creates a finding aid[32] in which increasing levels of detail are added as warranted. In other words, these descriptions move from the general to the specific. Finding aids that descend to the item level are the exception.

Archival catalog records and finding aids can be seen in aggregated resources such as ArchiveGrid.[33]

Sample questions:

- What level of detail is appropriate to describe a collection of digital videos from a public event?

- The laboratory data from this researcher is in fifty databases. How much detail is necessary to describe each one? What information should we include to describe the purpose of the research?

- How will users know whether one person ever corresponded with another if all names in the email are not included in the metadata?

- Is one metadata record sufficient for this complex website?

Conclusion

This essay has focused on ten areas in which archivists have expertise for making contributions to successful acquisition, appraisal, processing, preservation, and access to many types of born-materials library materials, whether or not the materials will be principally managed by or housed in the archives or special collections. An archivist is one of many experts with complementary skills who should work together to plan and manage digital initiatives.

The descriptions and sample questions for each of the ten areas reveal the tip of the iceberg of an archivist's expertise. If the institution does not take advantage of the archivist's array of skills, then others must become well versed in the issues if unpublished digital resources are to be acquired and overseen efficiently, effectively, and responsibly.

The digital content and formats that are appropriate for research libraries to acquire, curate, and provide access to, are expanding. As we move forward in this context, the inclusion of archivists in management of born-digital materials will help us meet the needs of creators, users, and research library digital professionals, today and into the future.

Notes

1. "Archivist" is used throughout this essay as shorthand for the full range of positions such as university archivist, manuscript librarian, and other professional staff who are trained to manage archival materials. Similarly, "archives" encompasses "special collections."
2. Erway, Ricky. 2010. *Defining Born Digital*. Dublin, Ohio: OCLC Research. http://www.oclc.org/content/dam/research/activities/hiddencollections/borndigital.pdf.
3. The Society of American Archivists' Digital Archivist Specialist (DAS) curriculum affords a sense of the range of skills archivists learn that are specific to management of born-digital materials. For the complete listing of DAS courses and instructors, see http://www2.archivists.org/prof-education/das/courses-and-instructors.
4. See, for example, Lavoie, Brian, Eric Childress, Erway Ricky, Ixchel Faniel, Constance Malpas, Jennifer Schaffner, and Titia van der Werf. 2014. *The Evolving Scholarly Record*. Dublin, Ohio: OCLC Research. http://www.oclc.org/content/dam/research/publications/library/2014/oclcresearch-evolving-scholarly-record-2014.pdf.
5. The Purdue University Archives policy for collecting websites is a good example: Bhatia, Ankur. 2013. *Purdue University Web Archive Collecting Policy: Virginia Kelly Karnes Archives & Special Collections*. West Lafayette, Indiana: Purdue University. https://www.lib.purdue.edu/sites/default/files/spcol/PurdueUniversityWebArchiveCollectingPolicy.pdf.
6. United States Copyright Office. 2014. "Chapter 1000: Websites and Website Content." In *Compendium of U.S. Copyright Office Practices, 3rd Edition*. 22 December. http://copyright.gov/comp3/chap1000/ch1000-websites.pdf. This interpretation was confirmed with Peter Hirtle, Senior Policy Advisor to the Cornell University Library, and an expert in copyright law as it relates to unpublished and archival materials (email communication, 12 February 2015).
7. Harvesting at scale is underway in a few nations, such as the UK, where legal deposit law enables the British Library to capture any website in the UK domain. See "Frequently Asked Questions For Webmasters." British Library. Accessed 13 May 2015. http://www.bl.uk/aboutus/legaldeposit/websites/websites/faqswebmaster/.
8. See, for example, the U.S. National Institutes of Health, "NIH Data Sharing Policy and Implementation Guidance." Updated 5 March 2013. http://grants.nih.gov/grants/policy/data_sharing/data_sharing_guidance.htm#app.
9. Some universities have websites to orient users to policies and services, such as this one at the Massachusetts Institution of Technology: http://libraries.mit.edu/data-management/.
10. See: Dearborn Carly, Amy Barton and Neal Harmeyer. 2014. "The Purdue University Research Repository: Hubzero Customization for Dataset Publication and Digital Preservation." *OCLC Systems & Services: International Digital Library Perspectives*. 30 (1): 15-27.
11. Telephone conversation with Sammie Morris, University Archivist and Head, ASC Division, and colleagues (Purdue University), 3 October 2014.
12. See, for example, Google's support pages regarding Gmail: https://support.google.com/a/answer/151128?hl=en.
13. IBM's product is one of many available examples: "Records and Retention." http://www-03.ibm.com/software/products/en/recorete.
14. Prom, Christopher. 2014. "Selected Email Preservation Resources." *Practical E-Records: software and tools for archivists* (blog). 4 April, in Research. http://e-records.chrisprom.com/selected-email-preservation-resources/.

15. More can be learned about each area here. See Pearce-Moses, Richard, 2005. *A Glossary of Archival and Records Terminology*. Chicago, IL: Society of American Archivists. http://files.archivists.org/pubs/free/SAA-Glossary-2005.pdf.

16. See Society of American Archivists (SAA) glossary definition of retention schedule: http://www2.archivists.org/glossary/terms/r/retention-schedule.

17. The Council on Library and Information Resources has published the most in-depth work in this area: Redwine, Gabriela, Megan Barnard, Kate Donovan, Erika Farr, Michael Forstrom, Will Hansen, Jeremy Leighton John, Nancy Kuhl, Seth Shaw, and Susan Thomas. *Born Digital: Guidance for Donors, Dealers, and Archival Repositories*. October 2013. Washington, D.C.: CLIR. www.clir.org/pubs/reports/pub159.

18. Copyright Law of the United States. http://www.copyright.gov/title17/.

19. See, for example, Cornell University's section on unpublished materials, "Copyright Term and the Public Domain in the United States." written by Peter Hirtle, updated 3 January 2015. https://copyright.cornell.edu/resources/publicdomain.cfm; and SAA's "Copyright and Unpublished Materials: An Introduction for Users of Archives and Manuscript Collections." Accessed January 2015. http://www2.archivists.org/publications/brochures/copyright-and-unpublished-material.

20. Some other types of value include administrative, fiscal, evidential, permanent and historical. The SAA glossary definition of appraisal reveals the term's complexity: http://www2.archivists.org/search/saasearch_glossary/value.

21. Some archival materials do have market value and warrant monetary appraisal. Examples include literary papers of high-profile authors and manuscripts that bear signatures of important historical persons.

22. National Institute of Justice. 2004. *Forensic Examination of Digital Evidence: A Guide for Law Enforcement*. Special Report No. 199408. Washington, DC: U.S. Dept. of Justice, Office of Justice Programs.http://www.nij.gov/publications/pages/publication-detail.aspx?ncjnumber=199408.

23. A wide array of tools is described in: Barrera-Gomez, Julianna and Ricky Erway. *Walk This Way: Detailed Steps for Transferring Born-Digital Content from Media You Can Read In-house*. 2013. Dublin, OH: OCLC Research. http://www.oclc.org/content/dam/research/publications/library/2013/2013-02.pdf.

24. Family Educational Rights and Privacy Act (FERPA): http://www2.ed.gov/policy/gen/guid/fpco/ferpa/index.html.

25. The Health Insurance Portability and Accountability Act of 1996 (HIPAA): http://www.hhs.gov/ocr/privacy/.

26. The California Public Records Act: http://www.leginfo.ca.gov/cgi-bin/displaycode?section=gov&group=06001-07000&file=6250-6270.

27. See, for example, the University of California at Irvine's rules for its virtual reading room: http://special.lib.uci.edu/using/access-priv.html.

28. Read, Richard. 2015. "Leaked University of Oregon letter Warns Professor to Immediately Return 22,000 Pages." Updated 26 January (7:20 AM). *Oregonian/Oregon Live*. http://www.oregonlive.com/education/index.ssf/2015/01/university_of_oregon_letter_in.html.

29. Association of Research Libraries, Coalition for Networked Information, and SPARC (Organization). 2012. *RLI 279, June 2012: Special Issue on Special Collections and Archives in the Digital Age*. Washington, D.C.: Association of Research Libraries. http://publications.arl.org/rli279.

30. Digital forensics tools are one such means. See, for example: Lee, Christopher, Kirschenbaum, Matthew G., Chassanoff, Alexandra, Olsen, Porter, and Woods, Kam. 2012. "BitCurator: Tools and Techniques for Digital Forensics in Collections Institutions." *D-Lib Magazine* 18 (May/June). doi:10.1045/may2012-lee.

31. For example, see: Jackson, Laura Uglean, and D. Claudia Thompson. 2010. "But You Promised: A Case Study of Deaccessioning at the American Heritage Center, University of Wyoming". *The American Archivist*. 73 (2): 669-685.

32. SAA glossary definition of finding aid: http://www2.archivists.org/glossary/terms/f/finding-aid.

33. ArchiveGrid: http://beta.worldcat.org/archivegrid/.

www.ingramcontent.com/pod-product-compliance
Lightning Source LLC
Chambersburg PA
CBHW061223270326
41927CB00024B/3483